MW00964428

On Retreat With ...

This new series, published by Medio Media/Arthur James, responds to the spiritual needs of people living today's busy and stressed lifestyle. Each book in the series is designed to allow the reader to develop a space for silence and solitude and spiritual practice in the context of ordinary life or by taking a short period of withdrawal. The structure of the book allows a flexible time-table to be constructed which integrates periods of reading, physical practice or exercise, and meditation.

Eileen O'Hea, a Sister of St Joseph of Brentwood, New York, is in private practice doing psychotherapy and spiritual direction, consulting with groups on team management and planning, and group facilitation. She also facilitates the teaching of Christian meditation and travels internationally giving retreats and work-shops on the integration of psychological and spiritual experi-ences of life. She is the author of *Woman: Her Intuition for Otherness*.

Also in the 'On Retreat With ...' Series

SELF AND ENVIRONMENT
Charles Brandt

ASPECTS OF LOVE
Laurence Freeman

THE MYSTERY BEYOND
Bede Griffiths

AWAKENING
John Main

The 'On Retreat With ...' Series

SILENT WISDOM, HIDDEN LIGHT

On Retreat With
Eileen O'Hea

MEDIO MEDIA / ARTHUR JAMES

LONDON AND BERKHAMSTED

First published in Great Britain in 1997 by

MEDIO MEDIA LTD
in association with
ARTHUR JAMES LTD
70 Cross Oak Road
Berkhamsted
Hertfordshire HP4 3HZ

A catalogue record for this book is available
from the British Library.

Unless otherwise stated, Scripture quotations are from the
New English Bible, copyright 1970 Oxford University Press
and Cambridge University Press

ISBN 0 85305 425 8

Typeset in Monotype Bulmer by
Strathmore Publishing Services, London N7

Printed and bound in Great Britain by
Guernsey Press Ltd, Guernsey, C.I.

Contents

Being on retreat:
how to do it yourself

Stay in your cell and your cell will teach you everything.
– Saying of the Desert Fathers

The problems of the world arise from people's inability
to sit still in their own room.
– Pascal, *Pensées*

Why set aside time for retreat?
Nature believes in retreats. Each day we virtually shut down our
active processes of mind and body for the retreat and renewal
we call sleep. Each year the animal and vegetable worlds go
through periods of deep rest we call hibernation. These are not
escapes from reality but ways of becoming more deeply attuned
to reality, respecting its ways and trusting the inherent wisdom
of nature.

Between each breath there is a moment of cessation, of deep
stillness, which is not the stillness of inaction but the stillness of
non-action. Between periods of daily work we naturally trust
the mind and body when they tell us to rest. Between two
thoughts there is an instant of mental silence.

On the London Underground, many stations have a rec-
orded announcement each time the train stops, warning

passengers stepping from the train to the platform to 'mind the gap'. Minding the gap is what this book is about – helping you, we hope, to see and respect the natural human need to retreat from action and speech at set times so that we can return to speech and action refreshed, re-balanced and renewed.

The spiritual life is not a specialized part of daily life. Everything you do in the day, from washing to eating breakfast, having meetings, driving to work, solving problems, making more problems for yourself once you have solved them, watching television or deciding instead to read, going to a restaurant or a movie or going to church, *everything* you do is your spiritual life. It is only a matter of how consciously you do these ordinary things, how attentive you are to the opportunities they offer for growth, for enjoyment, and how mindfully, how selflessly, how compassionately you perform them. Yet to live life spiritually all the time everyone needs to take specific times to focus on the spiritual dimension before everything else.

'Set your mind on God's kingdom and his justice before everything else, and all the rest will come to you as well.' Jesus said this in his Sermon on the Mount (Matt. 6:33). Taking a time of retreat will help you discover what he means by 'kingdom' and 'justice'. It will teach you that the kingdom is not a place but an experience of presence. The kingdom is within us and all around us. And you will learn that justice means balance, harmony, order. We hunger for justice in all the activities and relationships of our lives.

Buddhists see the spiritual significance of daily life in terms of ordinary mindfulness: doing everything with awareness, wakefulness. Christians similarly have long worked at praying at all times, giving glory to God in everything they do, practising the presence of God. This does not mean going around muttering prayers to yourself all day. You would only be more distracted in what you are doing. Nor does it mean thinking about God all the time. That would make you a religious fanatic. Praying ceaselessly, practising the divine presence is not something extra we do but the way we do whatever we are doing. It is a way of *being* in the midst of action: of being-in-action.

Perhaps the best comparison is with a relationship with someone you love. The awareness, the mindfulness, of that love surrounds and permeates you and all your words and responses all the day. You do not have to be thinking of the person you love all the time but they are with you and their often silent presence transforms your consciousness. Yet at the end of the day, or whenever opportunity allows, you return to the full presence of that person. Being with them helps the relationship to grow and deepen, even when romance wears thin. The 'quality times' together are essential for the health and development of love.

How to set up a retreat

The 'On Retreat With ...' series has been prepared to help you to spend quality time in the most fundamental relationship of your life, your relationship with God. In the ground of this relationship are planted all your human relationships, even your relationship with yourself. Quality time with someone requires a certain degree of exclusivity – you say *no* to other invitations and pleasant opportunities in order to concentrate on your presence with one person. Other jobs and responsibilities go on hold. When you return to address them you will be refreshed, calmer, and you can see the problems that easily overwhelm you in a better perspective. Retreat is not escape. You make a retreat in order to address reality more realistically and courageously. Retreat does not solve your problems but it helps you deal with them in a more peaceful and hopeful way. This is the meaning of a retreat: we retreat in order to advance deeper into the mystery of love's reality.

This book can help you structure your time and set the tone for the period of retreat you are allowing yourself to take. As life today is very busy and as it often seems impossible to find time for silence, stillness, and non-action, we need all the help we can get in order to take the time of spiritual retreat which both spiritual and psychological health require.

Time and place: your cell

You do not need to take a great stretch of time to make a retreat. But you need to designate a certain period of time and stick to it. It could be an hour, a morning or afternoon, a day, a weekend, a week, three months. In some traditions five-year retreats are customary. Let's start with a couple of hours.

If it is a short time, a couple of hours, you will probably be at home. Or you may have found you have some free time when away on holiday or a business trip. You do not have to fill in the empty space in the agenda: keep it empty. Go into the emptiness and you will emerge refreshed, more fulfilled. Set the time realistically. Put your answer-phone on. Turn the television or radio off. If you need to tell someone not to disturb you for the next couple of hours, do so. Put your work away or walk away from it. Then make a space.

The early Christian monks who lived much in solitude each had a cell. A monastic cell is different from a prison cell: you choose to be there. It is a place of stability, of security, of focus. It does not have to be elaborate. Cells are simple places. A chair, a cushion on the floor, a corner of a room. Make it tidy and clean. Set up a symbol of the presence; this could be a candle – ancient symbol of the presence of Christ – a flower, an icon, a photo, a cross, a Bible, or a simple everyday object. There should be a sense of simplicity, not clutter – of beauty, not prettiness. Have a watch or clock with a timer device nearby (not a loud ticker or too prominently placed).

With steadiness and ease: your body
Your retreat is a homecoming, an integrating, a remembering. It is not a spacewalk or a mind trip. You cannot come home unless you come inside, so take time to consider that you are also taking time to *make friends with your body*. And remember that you are only singling out the body for the purpose of the retreat. In fact you are really one single-woven tapestry of body–mind soaked and grounded in spirit: one being, fully alive.

Single out the body, then, and learn that it is happy to carry you, support you, hug you. It rejoices to pump blood, breathe, digest, walk, and sleep. It is a wonderful, mystical, funny contraption in which we are incarnated, and have epiphanies and transfigurations, and are crucified and resurrected.

Whatever you do on this retreat, keep breathing. Breathe as you take breakfast, as you go for a solitary walk or do some housework in your cell. Breathe while you are on the toilet. Breathe during your spiritual reading and as you doze off to a peaceful sleep after your day of silence.

You already have the three things necessary with which to make friends with your body. They are breath, gravity, and ground. You have been breathing since you were born and you will keep doing so as long as you need to. So relax and let breath breathe you. It is closer to you than your thinking. The way you breathe determines how you feel (see how your breathing changes when you are angry, frightened, or peaceful). As you give your attention to your breath you become naturally heavy. That is gravity hugging you. Give to it. Let it take you to the ground which stands under you (*understands you*). The

[11]

ground comes up to hold you, so relax and do nothing. In fact, un-do. Let it. You just pay attention to the breath as it breathes you in and out, in and out.

You might enjoy lying on your back before and/or after your meditation times, or after a walk. Lying on your back is an excellent way to start making friends with your body on this retreat. It helps turn off all the tapes playing in your head: tapes telling you to make a good impression on others, to be demure or macho, how to look sexy or respectable, how to dominate and be noticed. When you lie down, the three bony boxes of your body – the head, chest, and pelvis – stop chattering to each other for a while and relate directly to the ground instead. It is like turning gravity off for a moment.

Lie on your back with your knees bent so that your lower back is quite flat on the floor. Let your chin drop lightly towards your chest so that it is no longer pointing up to the ceiling. If this is difficult, put a folded blanket under your head, just an inch or so, no more. And stay, and wait in silence or listen to a taped talk on meditation or some music. If you doze off, so be it. When you do get up, first roll over gently on to your hands and knees. It is not helpful to yank the head straightaway in order to get up, because that immediately undoes all the work that breath, gravity, and ground have just accomplished in straightening you out and un-knotting you.

If you want to take this friendship with your body further, you could read *Awakening the Spine* by Vanda Scaravelli, *Yoga Over 50* by Mary Stewart (even if you are 25), and *Yoga and You* by Esther Myers. These three women are yoga teachers of great depth, humour, and insight.

Lectio: your mind and its emotions
Then, sitting comfortably, read a section of this book. Read

slowly. The book will last a long time, longer probably than your body. So there is no need to speed-read or devour the book and get on to another one. Re-read what you have read. Let your mind settle on a part of the passage which speaks to you most deeply. This may be just a phrase, a word, an image, or an idea. Revolve around that for a while. You don't have to analyse it. Savour it. The early desert monks called this *lectio*, spiritual (rather than mental) reading.

After a period of *lectio*, which can be ten or fifteen minutes, transfer your attention to the symbol which is the focal point for your retreat-space. Let your attention move towards the symbol, into the presence in the symbol. Let thought relax and the mind be still. When thoughts, fantasies, fears, anxieties, restlessness surface, let them come and let them go. Say, 'I'm sorry, you'll have to come and see me later. I'm busy doing nothing at the moment.' They will get the message if you give it strongly; be ruthless with them and don't compromise.

Meditation: going deeper
This would be a good time now for your meditation. Depending on how long you have been meditating or if you are just beginning, decide how many periods of meditation you are going to have during your retreat. A minimum would be two a day. Don't overdo it, but if you are a regular meditator you can profitably put additional periods in. More is not automatically better, of course. Three would be moderate. Six periods would be fine if you were sure you were not straining yourself or getting greedy.

Sit down with your back straight, sit still, close your eyes. Take a few deep breaths and then breathe normally. Then, silently, begin to repeat your word, your mantra. A good Christian mantra is the word *maranatha*. It means, 'Come, Lord,' or, 'The Lord comes,' but do not think of its meaning as you say it. Say the word simply and listen to it as you say it. This is the journey of faith, the deep listening. Faith leads to love. You could also take the word *Jesus* or *abba* (an Aramaic word used by Jesus, meaning 'father'). Whatever word you choose, stay with the same word throughout the meditation (and from one meditation period to the next) so that it can progressively take you deeper, from mind to heart.

Do not say the word with force. You are not trying to blank out the mind. Do not fight the thoughts which will come to you from every direction. Keep returning to the mantra. Say the word from the beginning to the end of the meditation whether you are aware of feeling distracted or peaceful. As soon as you realize you have stopped saying the word, start saying it again. In time (anywhere between five minutes and twenty years) the mantra will lead you at moments into complete stillness and silence, beyond itself. But if you are conscious of being silent then you are not yet completely silent, so keep on saying the mantra until the Spirit takes over. You will find that you say the mantra more deeply, more finely, more delicately as time goes on. Time your meditation with a timer – not too alarming a sound. If you are new to meditation, begin with twenty minutes (or less if you really find twenty too long). Otherwise thirty minutes is a good period to meditate for. If you have a gong, this will help lead into and out of the meditation peacefully.

After the meditation, come out slowly. Open your eyes. Pay attention to the symbol you have set up in front of you. This would be a good time to read some scripture. *The Burning Heart* would be a good book to use at this point – a collection of John Main's favourite Scripture passages with a short commentary by him. Again, read slowly, chewing and savouring the Word. Don't gulp it down. You could then listen to some music, do some yoga, draw, or paint.

Structuring your time of retreat

If you have to get back to work and daily life, take a few moments to appreciate the gift of present you have just enjoyed – let it go, be non-possessive. Read another section of this book, again slowly and savouring what appeals to you. Open yourself to the next thing you have to do and prepare to do it while keeping your mind and heart open to the presence you have just turned towards. Your prayerfulness continues into whatever you are now going to do. And you can share the fruits of peace and joy you have received with others, not by preaching, but in the way you relate to them. If you need to, pack up your retreat things reverently and get on with life.

If you have more time you can vary the elements of this retreat time. If you have a whole day, for example, you could schedule two, three, or four meditations. This will depend somewhat on your experience in meditation. Don't overdo it, and more does not mean better. If you are making the retreat with others, that will introduce another dimension of presence. Use this book together, reading it aloud. If you have a weekend or even longer you will need to schedule your time more carefully. Draw up a timetable but allow yourself to be flexible in keeping to it. Morning, midday, and evening are natural times for prayer – and before you go to bed. If you have a day or longer on retreat, do some manual work, even housecleaning, and get some exercise and fresh air. Walk in the garden or a park. Take this book with you and stop and read a section during your walk.

Don't just do something, sit there!

You might find the voice of conscience attacking you during your retreat. 'You are wasting your time,' it will say, or, 'You are being selfish.' You will think of all the practical, urgent, problematic things you could do. You will get an insight into a situation and want to dash off to implement it. Watch these restless thoughts and they will die down and return less frequently. This is why you will benefit from scheduling your time. It will fool your bush mind into thinking you are doing something productive. But your heart will teach you that you are not trying to produce or achieve anything. You are being. You are drinking deep, in the desert of modern life, of the waters of divine being. Your work and the people you live with, will all benefit from this time of retreat, so you are not being selfish. A gentle discipline in ordering your time of retreat – whether an hour or a day or a weekend – will help awaken a sense of inner freedom from anxiety, obsession, and fear. Enjoy it: find joy in it.

Laurence Freeman

Silent Wisdom, Hidden Light

Eileen O'Hea

I am grateful to Beatrice Bruteau, whose creative thinking in philosophy, theology and spirituality has inspired and influenced me through her books and publications.   *–EO'H*

Christian prayer, identity, and contemplation

When we speak of prayer in the Christian context we understand that this prayer must have something to do with Jesus – either he is the object of our prayer, or the example of it, or in some way he mediates or enables it. In Christian prayer, therefore, we encounter Christ in some way. This encounter may take us through a variety of phases as we get to know the person of Jesus at ever deeper levels. And as we get to know the person of Christ, we also get to know ourselves at deeper levels, at levels of identity not known to us before. In what follows I will be combining some of the work of Beatrice Bruteau with some of my own thoughts and reflections. This is a way of looking at the experience of some people in prayer; it is not presented as the only way.

What is prayer? In the Christian context it always has something to do with Jesus. Prayer is the lifting up of the mind and heart to God. Prayer in another sense is my turning towards the Divine Other, my total openness towards the Divine Other, my total attention, affections, and emotions turned towards the Other. In other words, all of me toward all of It. Christ in some way is the interspace in our prayer where our love and desire for God and God's love and desire for us are realized. Now as my being turns completely to the Divine Other, my prayer seems to go through different stages or phases. These stages are not necessarily sequential but they form one pathway into contemplative prayer where the experience of Christ is realized and we know that intimacy with divine life and love that we were created for.

One phase of this prayer is the prayer of *petition*. In this prayer I am in relationship to Jesus: I am asking something of him. I bring some of my problems or some need, and beseech Jesus to do something about it or them as he did in the Gospel stories. I want something from this person and in this phase of the prayer I'm not so interested in Jesus but what Jesus can do for me; my consciousness is centred on my personal need and gratification. I am so absorbed in my need that I don't see beyond it or see into Jesus yet.

Now if some of the my needs happen to get satisfied after I have brought them to Jesus, that might bring me to the second phase of my prayer, which is a kind of curiosity or fascination or *sense of awe*. This moves me from a private concern to an acknowledgment of the presence of anyone who can do such a great deed. Thus it puts me in touch with another kind of reality.

The third phase is the prayer of *appreciation*. I begin to notice that by looking at this person and appreciating his life I could gain similar goods for myself. Therefore if I want to improve myself, one way would be to imitate this Jesus, to study Jesus' character and actions in the situations in which he finds himself. In this phase of prayer I begin to compare what I do with what Jesus did. I might ask myself such questions as, 'What would Jesus do in this case? How would Jesus act in this situation?' What we can see here is that there is still something in this for me. Jesus is an object I am studying so that I can improve myself.

In the fourth phase, which we might call the prayer of *admiration*, there is a sense of going beyond myself: some of my self-consciousness gets lost even though Jesus is still an object of contemplation, just like a picture. If I am in a gallery I might look at a beautiful picture of a person, but it does not look back at me. Jesus now is a person I am looking at, but I do not experience Jesus looking at me. He himself is absent, so I still think and speak of him in the third person. He is wonderful, he is so good, he does this.

In the fifth phase it seems as if I begin to *speak to Jesus*. Jesus is no longer just a picture to me: I have face-to-face contact with him. This is the beginning of a personal relationship. I speak to Jesus and I begin to speak about myself to him. I begin to experience intercommunication; I am truly in relationship with a person, not an object. Now, as I start to experience this living contact, I begin to realize that what I am talking about, no matter how important it is, is not as important as the intercommunication that is happening.

Two things now result from this. First, the person who prays sees deeper into Jesus which is different from the picture or the story or the report or any analysis or lessons drawn from his life. I begin to experience a living reality which is life-giving. Second, contact with Jesus at this level awakens a deeper reality in me as well; my consciousness begins to expand. Now in Minnesota before a tornado a lot of sirens go off as a first warning of what is about to happen, and if there were such things in the spiritual life they would be happening at this stage of our prayer. Our self-consciousness and our world-consciousness are beginning to be tranformed as a consequence of this inter-relationship with the consciousness of Christ.

The second thing that happens at this stage is that people begin to think that they are finding their real self. They feel more rounded, or their consciousness is more expanded, and they experience their personality differently. We might feel forgiven or cleansed or saved or better, and this indicates something of the individual selfhood that is maturing somewhat and is coming into its own. Now we have no idea at this point that this self will go through a radical metamorphosis. At this point we think that the descriptive self *is* the self, and that we are enlarging it

[21]

and improving it; but that is not the case. We are also very aware that Jesus is other than who we are, that Jesus is outside of ourselves so to speak, and this in some ways affirms us.

As we move now to the sixth phase, or the prayer of *intimacy*, we move deeper into the light of Christ and let that light penetrate us. We experience deeper levels of reality within us, and the outward, human personality of Jesus seems to expand and fade as we enter more into Jesus' consciousness. A similar transformation is also going on in our own outward, human personality: it seems to expand and fade in us, and for that reason what we say and what we do, all those descriptive traits and qualities, seem to have less importance. This is because Jesus is communicating directly with who I am, passing through and beyond my behaviour and all the descriptive qualities. Now as these descriptive qualities melt away before the radiance of each person's central reality, the reality of who I am and the reality of who Christ is, so also the words that would capture them begin to fail us. What begins to happen is that silence seems to supervene as these two luminosities, these two balls of fire as it were, gradually grow together and become one. As I become one with the consciousness of Christ, it can no longer be said that I am looking at Jesus; rather, I am looking beyond all those descriptive qualities and I am regarding Jesus' living consciousness.

Now this next statement sounds rather convoluted but it is very important: the only way I can regard a living consciousness is to be conscious of what it is conscious of. Therefore at this stage of prayer we discover that we are looking to God and out to the world through the consciousness of Christ.

This brings us to the next phase of our prayer, which is when we are *one with the consciousness of Christ*. Then indeed living is praying and praying is living, because when I share the life of Jesus and Jesus shares my life, it is as though two lives have flowed together, or there is one life and two persons. There is no satisfactory way of describing it. In this phase of our prayer, the prayer of co- incidence, it is not a question of seeing the world through the consciousness of Jesus but of experiencing Jesus's own consciousness. If one is really going to unite with the person one loves one must become vividly aware of that person's sense of identity, because that is the most intimate thing about them. What was Jesus's experience of himself? One experience of himself was that he was the Beloved One, the very image of the Ultimate One with whom he is one. Now this experience is thrown open to the one who prays: I experience it as being true of myself so that I too hear the words spoken to me, 'This is my beloved one'.

St John of the Cross must have known this at a deep level of his being because he could freely say,

> Let us rejoice, beloved, and let us go forth to behold ourselves in your beauty that I resemble you in your beauty and you may resemble me in your beauty and my beauty be your beauty and your beauty be my beauty.*

In this we see that St John speaks as though there is a distinction and there is not a distinction; and both are true. This is what Beatrice Bruteau would call the 'prayer of insight', in which the subject sees or understands or loves an object. I see into the inmost reality of the object and know its deepest truth. The prayer of insight, therefore, is about our learning to live in God.

The prayer of manifestation is our experience of God living in us. In the prayer of manifestation I have a vivid sense of God's life being my life – not the most important thing *in* my life but God being the act of living which I am. So this coinciding with divine life and consciousness means, in the Christian

* *Spiritual Canticle*, stanza 36.

context, participating in the divine activity of creating. A prayerful life will always be an active life in the world. Love of God and love of neighbour have always been inseparable truths in the Christian tradition. Before, activity came about because of the nature, the condition, or the situation of the person praying. Now, it comes about because of the nature and will of God. I am impelled as it were to act; I am moved to act. Something deep within me rises up and causes me to want to go in a certain direction or to be moved in a certain direction according to that experience of the Spirit that I sense in myself.

In the prayer of manifestation, Beatrice notes four components. First, all my actions are God's actions. Now to the extent that I have become one with the consciousness of Christ, to that extent I am impelled to act because of the divine activity or the creative pressure that is now expanding and realized within me. A creative urgency is experienced as it moves through my limited ability and, no matter how limited my abilities, they are still filled with divine creativity. It's just as creative to make a good cup of soup as it is to produce a great art work, because all my activity is limited and yet all of my activity is divinely inspired.

The second component of this prayer of manifestation is the extension of the ministry of Christ. We feel that same urge to heal, redeem, and liberate as Jesus did. What was inside the mind and heart of God took form in Jesus and is now more realized in us; we participate in this very activity of God living in us. We have become the forms of the formless one. We are now that extension of Christ's ministry.

Thirdly, I participate in creating the world that I experience. In each of the gospel stories, before any cure there was a demand for faith. 'According to your faith be it done unto you.' I realize then at this stage of my life that my believing, the way that I experience faith, is integral to parts of divine manifestation in this world. I begin to see with the eyes of faith; I begin to see beyond all the descriptive qualities of person and our world, and can even say, with Jesus, 'Behold, the reign of God is at hand' – even in the midst of a very messy world. Because I have entered into the subjective consciousness of Jesus and have become one with it, I am also able to enter into the subjective experience of the other, so I know what it means when I hear, 'Whatever you do to the least of my sisters and brothers you do to me.' I now realize that we are all one.

Perhaps we never come as close to this in our daily life as when we extend compassion, when we become one with what is inside of the other and identify with the consciousness and experience of the other. This is just a little hint of what it is when we coincide with the consciousness of Christ. We are knowing the other from the inside.

Lastly in this prayer of manifestation I realize I can create new and better worlds. True prayer always moves us beyond ourselves to the Other, and all others, and so when Beatrice Bruteau writes about prayer she states:

> When the one who prays therefore is united with the Beloved but not simply collapsed in the realization that there never was anything except that one Being, this distinction is not due to a distance between Creator and creature but is the same kind of distinction that prevails inside the Godhead itself. The one who prays is no more separated from God than any one of the persons of the Godhead is separated from the other and similarly, the one who prays in the highest union is united with all the divine persons and they are united with one another.*

---

* 'Insight and Manifestation: A Way of Prayer in the Christian Tradition', *Contemplative Review*, Fall 1993, p. 28.

This, I think, was Christ's prayer in John 17:21 – '… that they may all be one. As you Father–Mother are in me and I am in you, may they also be in us …' – and this becomes our prayer.*

Many paths into this experience of Christ's own consciousness are part of Christian and contemplative prayer. The discipline of Christian meditation is one of these paths. It is a way into the experience of this participation in Christ's consciousness. Through our prayer we try through the repetition of a mantra and the stilling of our bodies to quiet our minds and hearts so that the descriptive self is no longer interfering or blocking us from that deeper realization where we are already at one and in union with the Beloved. As we persevere in our daily practice of morning and evening prayer, we notice that we begin to grow more peaceful within ourselves. We hope to notice as one of the fruits of our prayer that we begin to see or to know with the mind and heart of Christ. Perhaps in the beginning we only have small indications of this – perhaps we realize we are becoming more compassionate and can enter, at least a few more times a day, into the experience of another with true concern and true love. Or we may be more compassionate towards ourselves or more forgiving towards others and towards ourselves, or more aware of the goodness and beauty of others and of ourselves. The path of Christian meditation is a way into the experience of Christ's own consciousness because in it we let go of our self-consciousness which then allows us to be grasped by divine love and drawn into that experience of the living presence of God within us.

> If the contemplative is one who realizes participation in divine life then she or he must be someone who has on

* *The New Testament and Psalms: An Inclusive Version* (Oxford University Press, 1995), p. 173

dynamic

[26]

the one hand a commitment to poverty, to giving up identifying with the descriptive self and on the other hand the faith and the daring to accept identification with the true transcendent self which dwells in God and in which God dwells. When the sense of identity actually makes that shift in perspective then the contemplative breakthrough or insight is present and full. The contemplative life which is a union with the divine life must be creative. It is the nature and the vocation of the contemplative to create the world in the image of God as a circumsession of loving creative energies and as an ongoing process of ever-new improvisations.*

As we continue our reflection about becoming one with the consciousness of Christ, we are led to reflect further about contemplative prayer. When we speak of contemplative prayer we are naming an experience that happens to an individual on the level of person rather than the level of personality. The spiritual journey is a way of describing this happening in which an individual no longer locates his or her sense of identity at the level of descriptive qualities or personality. Rather they have been led, often by intuition, into a knowledge of a deeper reality or, to put it more correctly perhaps, of a consciousness which has no descriptors and cannot be contrasted. It is therefore called 'inarticulate consciousness' or 'contemplative consciousness'. Ordinary consciousness knows itself by contrast, by descriptions and by the things that it prefers or values. An example of this is someone who comes into my office and wants me to get to know them so they say, 'I am an INFP on Myers Briggs,' 'I'm a 2 on the Enneagram,' and 'I'm probably a passive aggressive

---

* Beatrice Bruteau, 'Contemplative Insight and a New Social Order', *Cross Currents*, Fall 1981.

personality.' Some describe themselves by contrast to others – 'I would never do what I see her/him doing.' Some might do it by the content of their life – 'I'm a mother, I have five children,' or, 'I'm a parish priest,' or, 'I'm a writer.' Some might describe themselves by some issue around which they have organized their life – 'I'm an over-eater,' or, 'I'm an adult child of alcoholic parents.' These are all descriptions of the self and as such tend to contain and limit the self.

Contemplative consciousness on the other hand is intensively absorbed by that which has no contrast so it cannot be described or evaluated. So when we speak of contemplation or a moment of contemplation, the person might try to describe it by such words as 'I was lost in silence,' 'I knew a oneness with God,' 'Everything was still.' But all of these descriptions are attempts to put in words what the person feels or thinks in reflecting on his or her prayer. True contemplation is an experience of unknowing: the person in the experience is not knowing anything at the time, because our ways of knowing come through our senses and other faculties. Contemplation, therefore, is a moment not confined by time, space, personality, intellect or emotions. It is an experience of a different consciousness which is the realization of oneness of being or oneness with the consciousness of Christ. It is not something known or experienced in the usual way, and therefore our words fail when we try to describe it.

Contemplative consciousness, or what is known as the contemplative moment in prayer, points to the reality of our identity, the reality of our being and divine being in the experience of union and love. This experience has always been part of Christian teaching and is expressed in several ways: that we are children of God, that we are created in God's image and likeness, that we are temples of the Holy Spirit, that the same Spirit that was in Jesus leading him through his life, death, and resurrection is in us leading us through our life, death, and resurrection.

This union with God, this experience of God's being and our being at one, is a reality in each of us. It is not something we work to attain; rather, it is something already present in us. We move toward it and open ourselves to this experience through prayer and through our commitment to the spiritual journey. It is true that this experience seems veiled in our awareness now, but it is one which grace makes available to us. Therefore, as we talk about identity we are not concerned with a narcissistic pre-occupation, or a psychological or emotional concern with de-velopment – although these are necessary for our spiritual journey. Rather, we are saying that our spiritual identity, the 'I', free of all descriptors, the 'I' knowing itself in God, is the foun-dation of all psychological, emotional, and intellectual under-standing and development. It could be said that all problems, personal and national, have their roots in our not realizing our true identity.

The spiritual journey is about relocating our identity as persons. It is the movement from the ego and ordinary con-sciousness (which describes itself by contrasts and by the things that it values) to the true self and contemplative con-sciousness. Now contemplative consciousness is intimately absorbed by that which has no contrast. It is a place where devotion and commitment are at their absolute peak, unsup-ported by any awareness of contrast. The contemplative person names Divine Life as the reality and then orientates his or her life and being around that reality.

All persons are called to contemplative consciousness. The movement towards this reality is called the spiritual journey. It is the movement from the ego to the true self. There are many paths to the contemplative experience but all contemplative paths will lead us beyond our ego, beyond claiming it with its

descriptions and contrasts. This ego is not the real 'me'; these paths will lead us into an experience of the true, contemplative self, the self we were created to be, the self that was made in the image of Divine Love.

In the Buddhist tradition the Zen teacher asked the student, 'What was your original face, the face you had before your parents were born?' It is this face that we discover as we travel along on our spiritual pilgrimage. Our whole psychological, emotional, and physical make-up identifies the self with the ego, its cravings, its desires, and its needs. Moving away from this place of identity means moving into what is unknown and only intuitively experienced. It is therefore a very difficult thing to do, and always involves commitment. But it is precisely because there is another experience, one we intuit – namely, a life free of fear, guilt, and anxiety, one in which the experience of loving, and of being loved for who we are, are ever-present realities. The Divine Love in us constantly calls us to itself, longing for us to experience this ever present, ever creating love that surges up from the depth of our being. Sometimes a veil that separates us from this reality gets pulled back and we glimpse this love and know it is worth our entire life, and know also that it is all that is. After such a moment, we construct our lives and lifestyle in line with this experience. This experience might come through some moment of prayer, or some insight received while meditating on sacred Scripture, or an event in our life, or a relationship of love, or a myriad of other experiences. No matter how big or small the incident, we know something we did not know before – not a new piece of information, but an experience of reality unknown to us before.

We say at this point that the person has been awakened. This awakening is wonderful because what the person sensed or desired or longed for is no longer a mere theological truth or an intellectual thought; it is now realized. On the other hand it is a confusing time because one can feel split. We have spent a lifetime constructing a world of meaning and experience around our ego as if it was the sum total of our being and all of reality. The discovery, not of a deeper level of ego consciousness but of completely different consciousness, can be quite awesome. It is something like our dream world. The world of the dream seems very real as we sleep. When we wake up we say, 'Oh, it was only a dream.' We don't entirely discount it, however, because we know that in it our unconscious minds are working things out. Our dreams are supplying us with important information about ourselves, but we do not live in the dream world. We use it, we respect it, but we get out of bed and go about the daily functioning of our lives.

The spiritual awakening of an individual is a process in which the person no longer identifies his or her sense of self with the world of the ego. A shift in where they locate their sense of identity begins to happen. Sacred scriptures of our own tradition as well as those of other traditions portray in a universal way our individual experience. In them we find that individuals had some direct experience of God or Christ which touched them at the very core of their being. They were engaged intellectually, emotionally, spiritually, physically; and they then sought ways to be true to this experience by creating doctrine and rituals which would help them live out what was known in them. The problem that we experience sometimes today with either doctrine or ritual is that they have lost contact with the original experience of Divine Life – Divine Love. When an awakening that profoundly touched the deeper self happens to an individual, he or she will also want to orientate their whole being – body, mind, and spirit – completely to the Divine Other. But we live in a world where identity is claimed by the ego, which is seen as the centre of reality, so this reorientation will be very difficult. It involves a radical change in our thinking, in our believing, on all levels of being. One example would be not identifying our sense of worth through the usual means. For example, not identifying my sense of worth with my feelings of importance, with my popularity, with the power that I yield, with the position that I have, with the authority that I have or with the reputation that I enjoy. These things might be there but they are no longer the source of my sense of identity.

Very often, people who are experiencing this will feel dissatisfied with many of the things that once satisfied and fulfilled them. So this involves a radical change in lifestyle and in perceptions of others as well. To know another consciousness is to know communion with the Divine Other and all others. Love of God and love of neighbour have always been inseparable truths in the Christian tradition. In this experience of known oneness I can no longer look up from the evening news or the morning newspaper and be content to shake my head at the plight of the poor, the abuse of women and children or the violence in Africa, Serbia or my own apartment block. These people are no longer objects of my concern or pity. No, now they are my brothers and sisters and it is a concern that is not momentary and left aside when I lay the paper down. I carry their pain in me and I must discern what I am to do with and for them. On a spiritual level the detachment from the ego might also mean letting go of some of those very comforting ways of praying or images of God that have brought us to this very moment. In our century with its emphasis on self-actualization, wholeness, physical and psychological well-being, the apophatic tradition as spoken about in classical mysticism seems countercultural and antiquated. Words such as 'renunciation', 'purification', and 'surrender' have with good reason (especially in women's experience) been identified with domination and control when they have been inappropriately applied.

The individual who has been awakened and then consents to pursuing this journey, who says 'yes' to the invitation of - Divine Love, will go through a transition period that is not unlike the purification period spoken about in classical mysticism. This transition period can last for minutes, weeks, months, or years each time we are invited into a deeper level of the experience of the mystery of God in us and in all creation. This transition, like all transitions, is filled with confusion, questions, doubts, and darkness. A decision in our ordinary life to change a job or anything else brings about similar experiences. It seems that right after we make the decision we wonder if we did the right thing: even if we were unhappy in the job, there was usually some security attached to it. Perhaps the people there or our familiarity with what we were doing gave us a feeling of confidence. As we move toward our new job, we are unsure. We don't know if people will like us, we don't know whether we will be able to do the job well enough, and sometimes we are afraid that we'll be found out, that we won't be as smart or as capable as our resumées made us seem. When we actually get to the job these questions lurk in our minds and we try with difficulty to get through each day. Gradually, though, we become acculturated to our new environment and perhaps after six weeks or six months we hardly remember that there was a transtion period.

The purification or transition that happens to one who moves towards contemplative consciousness is not dissimilar, but it happens on a different level and it can be frightening to us – not because something bad is happening but because when we embark on this journey we leave behind all the things that have buoyed us up and kept us linked with our egos. It feels as if we have nothing to hang on to, and this is frightening to people who have attached identity, meaning, and purpose to the things outside themselves. Contemplative prayer is an interior movement, a movement beyond ordinary consciousness. There are no props.

I do not see this period as a time when God snatches things away from us, as a parent might do for the child's own good; though indeed it might feel like that. Rather, I see this as a passage like a birth canal in which the desire and longing of the one awakened meets the desire and longing of God for the one awakened; mother/father God is there with us, bringing us into a place of new life, new consciousness. Sometimes in moments of prayer we become aware of this; sometimes this spiritual insight comes to us in the most ordinary circumstances of our life. It is a moment of knowing who we truly are. It is the discovery of our original face. So the sense of deprivation that was feared by the individual setting off on this journey is now seen to be illusion. They have discovered everything. Contemplative consciousness takes us beyond our ordinary consciousness and situates us in reality, in Divine Love. Contemplative prayer is a method of prayer that helps us prepare ourselves for this experience. In contemplative prayer we respond to the draw of Divine Love experienced in us and try to detach from all thoughts, all feelings, all images, all desires, even our desire for spiritual experiences or our desire for God, so that in stilling our minds and hearts the experience of Divine Love may well up in us unhindered by any preconceived notions of God, of love, of reality, of identity, or anything else. 'Be still and know that I am God' is very good advice here. The faculties of mind and heart and will are thus transformed by a reality other than that constructed by the ego; the transformation of consciousness begins. It is the transformed consciousness that allowed Paul to say, and allows us to say, 'the life I now live is not my life, but the life which Christ lives in me' (Gal. 2:20). In contemplative consciousness the duality that existed in ordinary consciousness disappears. The person now knows that the many are one, that there can be union yet differentiation, that death and resurrection are part of the same reality. This experience can be called 'communion consciousness', or 'contemplative consciousness', or 'mystical consciousness', or 'oneness with the consciousness of Christ'. All these phrases are trying to name a reality that is beyond articulation and to which all creation is called. This consciousness in us is the experience of knowing we are forms of the formless one, that Christ's healing, redeeming, and liberating activity in this world is now happening through us. It is the experience of 'communion consciousness' that makes us realize in a new way the meaning of 'whatever you do to the least of my brothers or sisters, you do to me'; and it is this experience of oneness with all creation with reality that teaches us not to dominate the earth but to unite with our earth, with Brother Sun and Sister Moon, with Mother Earth, with the dolphins, with the forest, with the seas, with the rivers, with our air, with the ozone layer, so that all creation may sing of the glory of God in us and about us.

> Christian hope can be expressed in images of birth and new life redolent of the experience of mothering. When human energy collapses Mother Sophia has the last word as she had the first and it is the word of life. With this same creativity and largesse by which in the beginning she brings into being the things that do not exist, she gives life to the dead with an outpouring of power that radically empowers. The beloved offspring return whence they came, mothered, into life.*

* Elizabeth Johnson, *She Who Is* (Crossroads, New York), 1992, p. 181.

Holy darkness, holy light

This chapter will explore what happens to us as we mature on the spiritual path of Christian meditation. The root of most, if not all, problems we experience is our not knowing who we really are; all problems, therefore, in this sense are spiritual problems. Our spiritual journey is about discovering our true identity. The work of this journey is to shift our centre of consciousness from the ego to the experience of the deeper self, or what we will call the true self. This shift does not happen easily because we have been conditioned since birth to experience ourselves through our ego consciousness. A leading psychologist of our time writes about this phenomenon:

> Accommodation to parental needs often (but not always) leads to an 'as-if personality' (Winnicott has described it as the 'false self'). This person develops in such a way that he reveals only what is expected of him and fuses so completely with what he reveals that – until he comes to analysis – one could scarcely have guessed how much more there is to him, behind this 'masked view of himself' (Habermas, 1970). He cannot develop and differentiate his 'true self' because he is unable to live it. It remains in a 'state of non-communication', as Winnicott has expressed it. Understandably these patients complained of a sense of emptiness, futility or homelessness for the emptiness is real. A process of emptying, impoverishment, and partial killing of his

potential actually took place when all that was live and
spontaneous in him was cut off.*

The experience of the true self has been put forward in
Christian teaching in statements in which our essential goodness
is identified and claimed. We have been taught that we are created in God's image, that we are temples of the Holy Spirit, that
the same Spirit that was in Jesus leading him through his life,
death, and resurrection is in us, leading us through our life,
death, and resurrection. In other words, we have been taught
that we are already in union with God. Now we have moments
of realizing these truths. At these moments we experience within ourselves a deep peace or sense of joy but as Alice Miller
states so well, most of us are not in communication with this
deeper reality, this true self; and because we identify with our
egos rather than our true self we live the greater part of our days
in the experience of anxiety, fear, guilt, or the sense that there is
something wrong about us or in us. In other words, we are
blocked from our true identity.

The blocks that keep us from the awareness of our true identity might consist of self-hatred, feelings of insecurity or infer-
iority, patterns or ways of thinking or feeling about ourselves
that make us feel not good, not whole, not worthy, not worth-
while. These are the conditions that our egos have seized on as
if they were the truth about us. What surrounds this experience
of the self and keeps it going is a system of denial.

Let me give you an example of how this system of denial
might work. Recently a friend of mine called to make a dinner
date. Because she travels a great deal and because of some
evening commitments I had, we had difficulty finding a time.

* Alice Miller, *The Drama of the Gifted Child* (Basic Books, New York, 1981;
Faber & Faber, London, 1983), p. 27.

We decided on a Monday night several weeks into the next month. On that Monday night I found myself at home, pleased at the prospect of having a night free. I had to look at my calendar for some reason and saw there the word 'dinner' and my friend's name. Instantly I thought, 'Oh, I put that on the wrong date,' and then erased it and wrote it in the box for the following week. The next Monday I went to the restaurant, sat at the table, and waited for my friend. Of course she never arrived since she had been there the week before and was probably now in another part of the country.

This is a minor and relatively unimportant incident, but it shows us a clever system of denial which has a propensity to maintain itself. I didn't want to know. I didn't want to be responsible for my friend's inconvenience, so I shoved it into the background and then acted as if the arrangement had never been made.

We see major instances of this system of denial in our day as we hear of people revealing and remembering at the age of forty or fifty some form of abuse they experienced in their early childhood. Something triggers their repressed memory and breaks through the system of denial that has kept them prisoners for so long. Part of the cleverness of this system is that it makes us feel comfortable in our discomfort. We have the illusion of safety and security. We think that there is no other experience and that this is reality.

We do many things in our daily life that keep us comfortable in our discomfort. For example, my friend Mary worries a great deal and is extremely anxious as she drives a certain road each day to her place of employment. I say to her, 'Mary, you don't have to go on this road. You don't have to take this long route; there is a simpler way.'

'No,' she replies, 'I know this route.' So she keeps choosing this route, choosing the discomfort that she knows because she

is afraid of experiencing something new or different or unknown. Some people keep on choosing patterns that are destructive to them. They might ward off intimacy when
intimacy is what they really desire and want in their life. They
might do this through a pattern of anger or avoidance which
keeps people at a distance from them. One possible reason
they cannot allow other more tender feelings is because they
feel more alive when they are angry. It is a pattern they have got
used to; they feel energized in their anger. To give this up
might mean experiencing a great emptiness. In another case,
giving up the experience of myself as a victim might mean that
I won't know who I am, and since I don't have any other experience of myself I fear that there might be nothing left for me.
The fear of experiencing this void in myself therefore prevents
me from getting in touch with my true self. In other words, we
can get stuck in some patterns, different ones for different
people. We get stuck in a way of seeing ourselves that keeps us
locked into an untruth about ourselves, keeping us unfree and
unhappy.

Now it was precisely because of this experience of the self, a
self chained to its false perceptions, that Jesus came into the
world and took on human flesh. Jesus takes on our wounds
because we have denied them. Jesus shows us the very place of
our denial. We deny our wounds, but Jesus puts them in front
of us. In reality these are our wounds that we are seeing in the
cross of Jesus, not just Jesus's wounds. Jesus is wearing them,
suffering them so that the system of denial that keeps us from
our reality can be broken through and we will finally accept our
wounds. Accepting our wounds breaks the system of denial and
brings about the process of our healing.

It is a wonderful experience for us when we know that
someone knows us and accepts us in our place of wounded-
ness. A woman who came to me in therapy had a disease which

doctors could not identify. Her husband was a doctor also. She said to me she wished those doctors and her husband were able to have some machine that would plug them into what she felt like just for a moment because she never felt really understood in her pain. Now Jesus is that person who fully understands and identifies with our wounds. Jesus is the one who takes these wounds on, who knows what we are going through, who fully absorbs our pain and our suffering and becomes one with us in it.

A young man whom I was seeing in therapy was very angry with his parents. His father was alcoholic and very disruptive in his family as he was growing up and this young man, Bill, carried this anger against his father with him all through his adult life. Finally, one day I had the parents come to my office with Bill and Bill explained to his parents how he felt, the anger he had and how he felt so dismissed, rejected, and misunderstood, especially about his father's alcoholism during Bill's teenage years. The father was a prominent business man who had in his later years stopped drinking and reorganized his life. He turned to his son and said, 'Son, if I did those things I am sorry but I don't remember.' Bill is still an angry man today, probably because he never quite felt understood even in this dramatic moment with his father. He never felt that his father understood his pain or had any idea of what he had gone through. If the father had taken on Bill's suffering to some extent, and was able to identify with the son and what had happened to the son because of his drinking, I am sure that Bill would have been able to begin the healing process that is so necessary to his life.

The cross of Jesus is essential in the experience of the person on the spiritual journey because it helps us know that we are met and accepted in the place of our greatest suffering. When we can allow this experience of Christ to release us from the bondage of our self-perception, from those blocks that keep us in our ego and that prevent us experiencing our true self, when we can allow this redeeming, liberating activity of Christ to penetrate us, then the healing process begins and we are freed from the experience of identifying with the ego. But we resist moving from this place; we help to maintain this system of denial because even though it is a place of suffering and discomfort we are afraid to leave it; we choose what is familiar to us instead. Some people who have experienced a deep depression, for example, are so afraid of returning to the experience of depression that they avoid having any reflective time in their life. They keep running or keep busy because they are terrified of going deeper into themselves and finding there only the bottomless pit which they experienced in depression. The spiritual journey is only superficially attended to because they have been duped into equating the black hole of depression with interiority and self-discovery. For them there are no flowers in the darkness, no darkness that can be sweet.

So too the spiritual journey feels risky, deathlike. It feels like going into a dark or unknown place if we leave a place of comfort – even though it's not a place that gives us a great deal of happiness or solace or life. People who pray contemplatively are shifting the centre of their consciousness from the ego and those images and beliefs about themselves, to the centre of reality where they are in union with God. If we pray contemplatively it means that we will dislodge some of the blocks that keep us from this reality, and these blocks will then surface into our consciousness. So the experience of contemplative prayer is also an experience of meeting some of the darker sides of our personality. They emerge and come into our conciousness because of our prayer. Many of us have the feeling that we used to be nicer people, or that we were able to keep the lid more securely on some of our thoughts or behaviours or feelings before we became more deeply involved in contemplative prayer.

For example, in my own life I find that years ago when I criticized things I used to think back and see how I did this or how I did that, whereas now I instinctively feel that what I'm criticizing is in my very self. Almost as the words are out of my mouth, I have the feeling that I am doing exactly the same thing that I am criticizing another person for. As we move more deeply into the contemplative experience we develop a heightened consciousness which brings an awareness of our behaviours, thoughts, and emotions. This is because whatever has kept us from the deeper self is being dislodged. Now, it is true that we also experience Christ meeting us at these places of our pain and darkness, giving us the grace, the insight, the spiritual consolation, or the experience of faith that will help us. As we pray and come into the reality of the deepest self, we must expect that the hidden things lodged in that place of denial will surface. I say this so that we will learn to be compassionate not just to others but also to ourselves. This emergence of our shadow side into conscious awareness indicates that we are getting further on our spiritual journey.

There was a teaching years ago that might still influence us, that said that the holier you became the more perfect you became. Now some of us are finding that that is not quite our experience. What seems to be happening to us is that the closer we come to the experience of Divine Love, the more we find ourselves unable to practise that love. We feel we are falling short, not measuring up; and so we become more sensitive to our own behaviours. This is part of the liberating activity of Christ in us. We also become more compassionate, less judgmental, more forgiving of others as well as of ourselves; and this indicates growth and maturity. So to know the contemplative experience, or to practise Christian meditation, means that we will know this mystery of death and resurrection in our lives. It is important for people who are praying contemplatively and practising meditation to know that the life cycles of the spiritual life are going on in us. There are times when we will have spiritual consolation and spiritual desolation around or after our prayer times. There are times of 'lights off', as Ruth Burrows says, and times of 'lights on'. These are the dynamics of the spiritual life, not perhaps part of the prayer experience itself but surrounding it.

Let us now consider the practice of meditation. When we ask people why they keep praying, they often respond, 'Well, it's a habit; it organizes my day,' or, 'I need quiet and this really gives me a time just to be quiet.'

These responses are certainly true and helpful, but they do not plumb the full depth of contemplative prayer. The practice of meditation is not just a routine act like brushing our teeth or doing some type of exercise. What causes us to pray is an experience of love; it is the response of an individual to the impulse of the Holy Spirit – or the impulse of love that is building up in us. Our response to this movement of the Spirit brings us back day in and day out to our meditation periods. This impulse of the Spirit, this growing awakening to the love that is within us, brings us to meditation in good times and in bad, in health and in sickness, on days when we feel like it and on days when we don't. It is not just that we put in the time, getting up to pray, and feeling a little better. No: what we discover in our prayer is a relationship of love and intimacy. We become awake to reality. This experience of love may or may not overflow into our emotions. It is an experience of the interior senses. It is an experience of knowing, independent of any external sense or any emotion. We know we are loved, we know God is love, we know we want to be in a relationship of love with Divine Love.

Now, what exactly do we do when we pray? Let me use an example from my childhood. I grew up in the city and I would return from school to my home for lunch each day. I would go upstairs and enter a hallway where there was a cloakroom at one end. I would take off my coat, boots, and hat, and hang them in the cloakroom. Then I would go into the house where my mother was waiting for me. She would have my lunch ready on the kitchen table and we would both sit down and talk and eat. Now, in the practice of Christian meditation also there is something like a hallway. Here we hang up those thoughts, feelings, and emotions not because they aren't valuable or important but because these things will be attended to when we have finished our prayer. At this point we are clearing our minds of those things even though they are important and do need our attention. In contemplative prayer, we are responding to the impulse of the Spirit that is in us; we are allowing all our energies to return to home base, as it were. In our prayer time we are, in effect, directing our whole selves toward Divine Love. We are placing ourselves in light and love. Our consciousness and its energies are drawn into the experience through the practice of the mantra which helps create the environment where the deeper self is realized. This letting go of thoughts, emotions, and experiences, and going into that place of love, is not the act of a person who is in a stupor; nor is it an act that is so routine that we hardly know that it is happening. Rather, it is the practice of a person with an awakened heart. It is a practice of heightened consciousness, a consciousness that allows itself to be informed by a deeper reality, that allows itself to be situated, totally, in that reality. Sometimes the person who has been on this path for some time has different experiences. True contemplative prayer, however, is an experience of unknowing. Once we begin to know our experience then we are no longer in a truly contemplative experience, because the contemplative experience takes us beyond our ordinary ways of knowing and experiencing things.

Sometimes as we say the mantra we notice that it is more

difficult and we are more restless, less peaceful, in repeating it. At such times we must continue to allow our energies to be drawn into the experience of the prayer word that we are using, because that is the environment of love that will carry us into the union of our being with the being of God.

We are not looking for experience when we pray, but on some days our prayer seems to take a long time. At some time during our prayer we might wonder, 'When is that bell going to go off?' or, 'When is this time going to be finished?' On another day we might hardly notice the time going by. All of this is part of the spiritual journey. There are moments during our prayer times when it takes energy and will and commitment to stay in our prayer. There are other days when the time goes quickly, or we might experience a sense of joy.

This experience can be likened to a friend of mine who wears a certain kind of perfume. If I go into a room after she has been there I say, 'Ellen must have been here – I can smell her perfume.' Sometimes in our prayers there is not an experience that we give our attention to during the time of our prayer but when we finish our prayer something in us seems to have got connected with something deeper, and there is a lingering response in our bodies and our emotions to what has been experienced during our prayer time.

Over a period, those who pray contemplatively may notice a heightened consciousness, because their consciousness is shifting from the ego to the deeper self. They might say that they feel more detached, more at peace, more alert. They might feel more awake even to the sounds around them, more alert to the things seen on television. For example, they might have more difficulty watching anything that hints at violence on television. At one time they could have watched certain programmes, but now they find they no longer enjoy them because the centre of consciousness is moving to resting in

Divine Love and it cannot tolerate violence or pain inflicted on others.

Another thing we notice on the spiritual journey is that there can be an overlapping of what is happening to us spiritually and psychologically. Sometimes we can experience things quite separately but at other times the lines so to speak overlap. Sometimes a person can come for therapy and know a real depression or dark experience in their life, but at the same time spiritually they feel a great peace and recognize that this is just something they have to go through. At other times these two things come together: psychological and spiritual darkness merge. Some people speak of this as being in a tomb or a deep hole, feeling that there is no way out, and they feel that God is absent.

When people come for spiritual direction and are in one of these dark places, the director explores with the person several possibilities: Is this experience part of the death/resurrection mystery or process of transformation which is inherent in the spiritual journey and in this individual's maturing faith? Is it some form of depression arising from a psychological or chemical root? Or is it the result of some resistance within the individual's life? If it is discerned that the person has this death-like experience because this is what happens immediately before new life or transformation, the director encourages the person to remain committed to prayer despite the dryness or desolation. Usually such individuals are comforted because someone has helped them identify their experiences, and because they now see them as a normal part of this maturing in faith. I might note here that some of their relief also comes from realizing that they did not do anything wrong or bad to cause their discomfort or their sense of God's absence. They are also reminded that the sense of God's absence, however disconcerting on an emotional and psychological level, is not a reality. It is the world of the ego and its judgment that make it seem so. The truth is that we are in union with God. Sometimes we experience this in our bodies and emotions and sometimes we don't. Those who have travelled on this journey over time know that neither experience is particularly important. The mature person of faith does not fasten on such experiences, but recognizes them and allows them to be what they are. The mystics, for instance, saw darkness and light as flowers of the same garden and were able to find comfort in both. The individual and the director might also discern that the experience of being in a black hole is the result of psychological depression, in which case the individuals should seek psychological help as well. How they handle the disease of depression, or any difficulty in their life, is an integral part of the spiritual journey. They are part of the crisis of limits we humans know, part of our human conditioning, and like Jesus we must live with our flesh, accept our flesh, be open to its possibilities, its gifts, its limits, and learn how to work with our flesh and to do those things that will be helpful to us psychologically, emotionally, and spiritually.

The death/resurrection mystery is a constant theme in our lives and becomes more conscious as we detach ourselves from things we cannot change, and accept our finiteness. Maturity in faith, however, brings us to the realization that the true self is not dependent on any external happenings or events for its realization of its own inherent goodness, lovableness, and worth. It is not dependent on how well our bodies function or how well our minds function. We too are like the flowers in the darkness. Hidden beneath our finite flesh is our capacity for infinity. Hidden beneath our personality is our person, our essential nature. Hidden beneath our autonomy is our capacity for communion.

The third thing the director and the individual discern is:

the individual's sense of darkness, sadness, depression coming from some form of resistance? In other words, is the individual warding off some impulse of grace or the activity of God calling them to something new? Is there something that wants to surface into consciousness that the individual is resisting? Perhaps we are being called to forgive someone and we don't want to look at that; or maybe we have a problem with alcohol that we won't allow into our full consciousness so we ward it off. Warding off self-knowledge and truth in any of its forms is warding off grace or locking out divine light. This is resistance. Since my spiritual life and my personal life are in continuous dialogue with each other, my closing-off in one area will affect the other. I cannot go to prayer totally open to Divine Love and its activity and be warding off the impulses toward forgiveness or reconciliation in my personal life that are this Love's activity in me. I cannot be engaged in destructive or self-abusive behaviour in my personal life and at the same time believe that I can be totally open to divine love in prayer – as though my personal life and my prayer life were two separate entities.

Now in my prayer I might be struggling to deal with what I am being called to in my personal life, but I am trying in my prayer to be open to that impulse. If I am not, this accounts for the experience of resistance that we have in our prayer. We resist prayer because we are being called to new growth, to transformation, to allowing into our consciousness some truth that will invite us to change. Since the ego sees all change only as an experience of loss and death we resist change by resisting total openness or detachment during our times of prayer. This is what we label as being stuck or in a rut. Ruts are not lifegiving but they are familiar patterns to us. Like my friend Mary, who doesn't want to change her driving pattern even though another route would be easier, we choose the discomfort of our resistance because we are duped by our egos into believing that this path is easier than the change we are called to. Some form of death (or, in other words, some form of detachment from our egos) always precedes the experience of new life; but because the life we will experience is new, we cannot imagine it.

The disciples had this problem with Jesus. They could not imagine life after death, so they could not believe in it. In daily life, forgiving someone who has hurt us presents us with this death/resurrection mystery. We hold onto the hurt because we believe the other has taken something from us: perhaps our peace, our good feelings about ourselves, our reputation. As long as we believe they have this power, the thought of forgiveness terrifies us; we imagine them usurping this power over us again, if not now then at some future time; or we imagine that this peace at our centre can easily be taken from us. Then we are condemned to live very threatened lives, and cut off from full communcation with ourselves and with the other. Those who can extend forgiveness to others are able through prayer and discernment to centre their consciousness in the reality of the true self. They realize that no personal diminishment is possible, that nothing can be taken from them because they already possess everything. On this level they are one with Divine Light. This is, so to speak, the resurrection of the body in this world. It is an experience of liberation, of knowing a reality so deep within me that no external person or thing can diminish this experience of the self, this reality of my being at one with Divine Being. It is an experience of freedom. This is what the daily experience of the death/resurrection mystery leads us to.

Each time we detach ourselves from our ego we experience new life. The spiritual director encourages the individual, therefore, to make this resistance conscious. When this resistance is brought into the light of consciousness, we are able to deal with it effectively. We are able to uncover the ego's involvement and to make choices for new life. Life, we must remind ourselves, is a process, a gradual unfolding of our true identity.

Undoing our resistance in any area of our life is a process too. That is why we try to be as compassionate and patient with ourselves as God is with us. That is why we keep returning to our practice of meditation and wanting to be totally open to Divine Life. We know our egos may resist this life, but the very act of returning to prayer is living out our affirmation of Divine Love. The rays of this Love, its light and its warmth, will enable us to detach ourselves from our ego.

Our times of prayer are the reminders we give ourself of Christ's resurrection presence in every aspect of our life. In other words, we realize that we are not alone in this. This is the healing, redeeming and liberating activity of Christ in our life.

The person who prays contemplatively will experience continual death and resurrection. This experience is usually manifested in daily life and is not obvious in our times of meditation. However, there might be little hints or references that we become aware of as we leave our prayer periods and return to the hallway. When we return to the hallway, we go back to where we hung those things that need our attention, and we gather them up. Because our minds and hearts have rested in Divine Energy our perceptions are that much clearer. Our minds and hearts have been influenced by resting in this energy. We are changed by the practice of our prayer. Seeing differently is one of the fruits of our prayer.

Other fruits of our prayer are experiencing faith at ever deeper levels, knowing the vigour of hope, participating in a love that is pure and universal, and extending the love and peace that we have experienced. We leave the hallway of prayer and return to daily life, to the market place, because true contemplative prayer will always lead us beyond ourself to the Other, and all others, in love and service:

'There exists in all beings,' says Teilhard, 'a common centre' through which 'they meet together at a deeper level ... and we may call this Centre equally well the *point* upon which they converge, or the *ambience* on which they float....' This bond of unity constitutes the '*axis* of all individual and collective life. It is in virtue of this axis that we see that Christ has not only a *mystical*, but a *cosmic body*.... And this Cosmic Body, to be found in all things, ... is imminently the *mystical Milieu*; whoever can enter into that milieu is conscious of having made his way to the very heart of everything, of having found what is most enduring in it.*

This is the experience of contemplative consciousness, a consciousness that knows the interrelationship of all things, a consciousness that knows itself as participating in Divine Life and therefore does what Divine Love does, by giving itself in love to the Other and to all others.

* Beatrice Bruteau, *Evolution toward Divinity: Teilhard de Chardin and the Hindu Traditions* (Theosophical Publishing House, Wheaton, illinois, 1974), pp. 55–6, quoting Teilhard, *Letters from a Traveller*, p. 45.

The World Community
for Christian Meditation

Meditation in the tradition of the early Christian monks and as John Main passed it on has led to the formation of a world-wide community of meditators in over ninety countries. Weekly groups meet in many kinds of places and number over a thousand. An International Directory is maintained at the Community's London International Centre. A Guiding Board oversees the direction of the Community, a quarterly newsletter, the annual John Main Seminar, the School for Teachers, and the co-ordination of the Christian Meditation Centres around the world.

Medio Media

Founded in 1991, Medio Media is the publishing arm of the World Community for Christian Meditation. It is committed to the distribution of the works of John Main and many other writers in the field of contemplative spirituality and interfaith dialogue. Medio Media works in close association with the British publisher Arthur James. For a catalogue of books, audios, and videos contact Medio Media Ltd at the International Centre in London.

Christian Meditation Centres

International Centre
>International Centre
>The World Community for Christian Meditation
>23 Kensington Square
>London w8 5HN
>Tel: 0171 937 4679
>Fax: 0171 937 6790
>e-mail: 106636.1512@compuserve.com

Australia
>Christian Meditation Network
>P.O. Box 6630
>St Kilda Road
>Melbourne, Vic. 3004
>Tel: 03 989 4824
>Fax: 03 525 4917

>Christian Meditation Network
>B.O. Box 323
>Tuart Hill, WA 6060
>Tel/Fax: 9 444 5810

Belgium
>Christelijk Meditatie Centrum
>Beiaardlaan 1
>1850 Grimbergen
>Tel: 02 269 5071

Brazil

Crista Meditacao Comunidade
CP 33266
CEP 22442-970
Rio de Janeiro RJ
Fax: 21 322 4171

Canada

Meditatio
P.O. Box 5523, Station NDG
Montreal, Quebec H4A 3P9
Tel: 514 766 0475
Fax: 514 937 8178

Centre de Méditation Chrétienne
Cap-Vie
367 Boulevard Ste-Rose
Tel: 514 625 0133

John Main Centre
470 Laurier Avenue, Apt 708
Ottawa, Ontario K1R 7W9
Tel: 613 236 9437
Fax: 613 236 2821

Christian Meditation Centre
10 Maple Street
Dartmouth, N. S. B2Y 2X3
Tel: 902 466 6691

India

  Christian Meditation Centre
  1/1429 Bilathikulam Road
  Calicut
  673006 Kerala
  Tel: 495 60395

Ireland

  Christian Meditation Centre
  4 Eblana Avenue
  Dun Laoghaire, Co. Dublin
  Tel: 01 280 1505

  Christian Meditation Centre
  58 Meadow Grove
  Blackrock, Cork
  Tel: 021 357 249

Italy

  Centro di Meditazione Cristiana
  Abbazia di San Miniato al Monte
  Via Delle Porte Sante 34
  50125 Firenze
  Tel/Fax: 055 2476302

New Zealand

  Christian Meditation Centre
  P.O. Box 35531
  Auckland 1310

Philippines

5/f Chronicle Building Cor. Tektite Road
Meralco Avenue / Pasig
M. Manila
Tel: 02 633 3364
Fax: 02 631 3104

Singapore

Christian Meditation Centre
9 Mayfield Avenue
Singapore 438 023
Tel: 65 348 6790

Thailand

Christian Meditation Centre
51/1 Sedsiri Road
Bangkok 10400
Tel: 271 3295

United Kingdom

Christian Meditation Centre
29 Campden Hill Road
London w8 7DX
Tel/Fax: 0171 912 1371

Christian Meditation Centre
13 Langdale Road
Sale, Cheshire M33 4EW
Tel: 0161 976 2577

Christian Meditation Centre
Monastery of Christ the King
Bramley Road
London N14 4HE
Tel: 0181 449 6648
Fax: 0181 449 2338

Christian Meditation Centre
29 Mansion House Road
Glasgow
Scotland G41 3DN
Tel: 0141 649 4448

United States

John Main Institute
7315 Brookville Road
Chevy Chase, MD 20815
Tel: 301 652 8635

Christian Meditation Centre
1080 West Irving Park Road
Roselle, IL 60172
Tel/Fax: 630 351 2613

Christian Meditation Centre
322 East 94th Street No. 4B
New York, NY 10128
Tel: 212 831 5710

Christian Meditation Centre
2321 South Figueroa Way
Los Angeles, CA 90007-2501

Christian Meditation Centre
1619 Wight Street
Wall, NJ 07719
Tel: 908 681 6238
Fax: 908 280 5999

Christian Meditation Centre
2490 18th Avenue
Kingsburg, CA 93631
Tel: 209 897 3711

Hesed Community
3745 Elston Avenue
Oakland, CA 94602
Tel: 415 482 5573

Meditation on the Internet

WCCM.Archives
The WCCM, in collaboration with the Merton Research Institute
(Marshall University, USA), has archived a number of files: how to
meditate; biographical information on John Main, Laurence Freeman,
and others; International Newsletters; catalogues of books, audio-
tapes, and videotapes; the Rule of St Benedict and Benedictine
oblates; the International Calendar of events; John Main Seminars;
New Testament sources; and more. The Index of files and all individual files may be retrieved by anonymous FTP or the WWW using
the following URLs:

ftp://mbdu04.redc.marshall.edu/pub/merton/wccm/
http://www.marshall.edu/~stepp/vri/merton/wccm.html

The URLs for the Merton Archives are:

ftp://mbdu04.redc.marshall.edu/pub/merton/
http://www.marshall.edu/~stepp/vri/merton/merton.html

Merton-L is a forum for discourse on contemplative life. To subscribe, send e-mail to

listserv@wvnvm.wvnet.edu

containing the single line of text:

subscribe merton-l yourname

(substituting your real name for yourname, of course).

WCCM Forum
The WCCM.Forum is an outgrowth of the WCCM.Archives. Again,
in collaboration with the Merton Research Institute, the expressed
and sole purpose of the WCCM.Forum is to provide a place for sub-
stantive discussion on the daily practice of Christian Meditation as
taught by John Main, the works of John Main and Laurence Freeman,
and the work of the WCCM in general.

T6: WCCM, John Main, Laurence Freeman
In keeping with the expressed purpose of the WCCM.Forum as described above, posts about other types of meditation should not be
posted to the T6 channel of Merton-L. (See the Merton-L faq for
information about discussions on other channels.) Posts to T6 are
moderated by the Merton-L owner(s) and are also monitored by T6
discussion leader, Gregory Ryan, who is the archivist of the WCCM

electronic files. Questions or comments of a personal nature or suggestions concerning T6 may be submitted to Greg via e-mail:

gjryan@aol.com.

To subscribe to T6
To join the channel one must be a present member of Merton-L or, if not, subscribe to it. To subscribe to Merton-L, send e-mail to

listserv@wvnvm.wvnet.edu

containing the following single line of text:

subscribe merton-l yourname

(substituting your real full name for yourname, of course). Anyone who has subscribed to Merton-L may join the WCCM channel by sending e-mail to

listserv@wvnvm.wvnet.edu

(from your subscription address) containing the following single line of text:

set merton-l topics: +T6

Also in this series:

The Mystery Beyond

In this retreat, **Bede Griffiths**, one of the great spiritual forces of this century, guides us to a deeper insight into the reality of our spiritual quest. He addresses the dangers of fundamentalism and intolerance in all religious traditions and shows how meditation opens us to the transcendent unity of the non-dual – where we are ourselves but know ourselves to be one with all others. In the light of this experience he goes on to reveal his exciting and prophetic understanding of the church and its purpose in the world.

Bede Griffiths (1907–93) is recognised by leaders in all religious traditions as one of the prophets of the twentieth century. A Benedictine monk, he left England to spend the last forty years of his life in India where, he said, 'he discovered the other half of my soul'. His autobiography *The Golden String* and his later book *The Marriage of East and West* show how truly he pursued his call to be a bridge between spiritual traditions.

'The whole of humanity constitutes in principle the mystical Body of Christ … but the Christian revelation does not deny that the divine mystery is present in different modes, different expressions, different symbols, different languages in different parts of the world.'

Aspects of Love

In this retreat **Laurence Freeman** explores the central value of all essential spiritual life. Love matters to us all. But what does it mean and how can I learn to love – and to allow myself to be loved. Love of self, of others and of God: these are the Aspects of Love which Laurence Freeman describes as our way of experiencing the simplicity and richness of love. He offers simple but surprising insights into how we can enter love's reality more wholly.

Laurence Freeman is a Benedictine monk of the Monastery of Christ the King, London, and Director of The World Community for Christian Meditation, a global contemplative network inspired by the teachings of John Main.

'What finally heals the wounds of self-division is love. Love unifies, unites and overcomes the wounds of our alienation and simplifies us.'

Self and Environment

Writing from his hermitage in the forests of British Columbia, **Charles Brandt** leads us in this retreat to a fuller sense of the sacredness of creation and of our oneness with nature. He explores the damage inflicted on our sense of self and of God by the split we have made between humanity and the natural world. He helps us recover wholeness by showing how meditation and insight into the beauty of the world offer vital hope for a world in crisis.

Charles Brandt was trained as an ornithologist and environmentalist before being ordained as a hermit priest in British Columbia. He occasionally leads retreats which share the fruit of his solitude.

'My hermitage is located deep in the temperate rain forest on the Oyster River. The logging road along with other trails through the forest is where I practice walking meditation. I do not think of the road as leading anywhere. It is the road to nowhere, the path on which I journey and have been journeying for a lifetime ...'

Awakening

John Main guides this retreat with inspiring insights into essential spiritual experience. Beginning with the interior revolution called 'conversion', he explores the way of meditation as a deepening encounter with the person of Jesus and the mystical reality of the church as a community of love. The retreat talks are accompanied by helpful questions which allow these great questions to penetrate our own personal experience.

John Main (1926–82) was a Benedictine monk whom Bede Griffiths once acclaimed as 'in my experience, the best spiritual guide in the church today'. John Main's books and live-recorded talks continue to guide many around the world to deeper spirituality and also to inspire inter-religious dialogue on many fronts.

'The first thing to understand is the wonder and marvel of silence as a path into the mystery of being. Worship is impossible without silence because once we come into the presence of the mystery all we can do is bow and bend low.'